Fade Street

MARK GRANIER's first collection, *Airborne*, was published in 2001. He won the Vincent Buckley Poetry Prize in 2004 and was awarded Arts Council Bursaries in 2002 and 2008. His second collection, *The Sky Road*, was published in 2007.

Also by Mark Granier

The Sky Road (Salmon, 2007)
Airborne (Salmon, 2001)

Fade Street

Mark Granier

London

PUBLISHED BY SALT PUBLISHING
Fourth Floor, 2 Tavistock Place, Bloomsbury, London WC1H 9RA United Kingdom

All rights reserved

© Mark Granier, 2010

The right of Mark Granier to be identified as the
author of this work has been asserted by him in accordance
with Section 77 of the Copyright, Designs and Patents Act 1988.

This book is in copyright. Subject to statutory exception
and to provisions of relevant collective licensing agreements,
no reproduction of any part may take place without the written
permission of Salt Publishing.

Salt Publishing 2010

Printed in Great Britain by the MPG Books Group, Bodmin and King's Lynn

Typeset in Swift 9.5 / 13

for my wife, Sam (for everything)

This book is sold subject to the conditions that it shall not,
by way of trade or otherwise, be lent, re-sold, hired out,
or otherwise circulated without the publisher's prior consent
in any form of binding or cover other than that in which
it is published and without a similar condition including this
condition being imposed on the subsequent purchaser.

ISBN 978 1 84471 736 1 hardback

1 3 5 7 9 8 6 4 2

Contents

Sing, Words	1
A Photograph Of Fade Street, Dublin, 1878	2
Warmer	3
Plain Song	5
False Memory	6
Naylor's Cove	7
Skull	8
Bicycle Seat, Bull's Head, Bull-Leap	9
Portraits Of A Grouse-Beater, 1975	10
Found Landscape	12
At The Butcher's In Colmenar	13
At Sea	14
Section	15
The Older Standing Army	16
One Of The Houses James Joyce Lived In, Once	17
Ghost Story	18
On An Empty Can Rolling In The Night A Week After Your Death	19
The Chaos Ripple	20
The Doctor	21
Eclipse	22
Night, Wind, Dead Leaves	23
Wake	24
A Chest Of Drawers	25
Outside, In	26
Crest	27
Pocket Venus	28
There's Probably No God. Now Stop Worrying And Enjoy Your Life	29

Breasts	30
Fruit Bats In Sydney	31
1. *Evening, Port Elizabeth*	31
2. *Afternoon, Botanic Park*	31
On The Sky Road To Malaga	32
New Year's	33
Critic	34
Stopwatch	35
Later Days	36
Three Riddles And A Limerick	37
After Li Po	38
The Far Side	39
Dark Mutter	40
Dream	41
Lookout	42
The Last Wolf In Ireland	43
'Don't End With History Or The Sea'	44
Handholds	45
Departures	50
Colum Cille's Derry	50
The Bell	50
Oisín Remembers	50
The Hosting	51
Payment In Kind	51
Among Trees	52
The Yes Man	52
The Terror	52
Memo	53
Notes	54

'If your eyes stop moving you're dead.'
— DAVID HOCKNEY

Acknowledgements

Acknowledgements are due to the following publications where some of these poems, or versions of them, first appeared: *The Irish Times*, *Poetry Ireland Review*, *The SHOp*, *The Cork Literary Review*, *The Wolf* and the anthology, *Salmon: A Journey In Poetry*; also two web-based outlets: George Szirtes' blog and Paul Perry's 'The Workshop'. My special thanks to Séan Lysaght, Ian Duhig, Chris Stevens, Joseph Woods, Yvonne Cullen and Patrick MacAllister for their invaluable suggestions.

I am very grateful to An Chomhairle Ealaíon/The Arts Council for a Literature Bursary in 2008.

Sing, Words

That you may survive
those star-grazed years after I've
gone back to where I'm going: air

of a song, dead air, my dark star
set in the glimmerless hush,
cool enough to touch.

Sing, that something remain
of these epic, mundane
conversations hoofing it down my back

clicketty clack—
that you may hit or miss
with a flourish, a backdraught, a hiss

like intaken breath. Life itches to get out
of its mildewed coats,
glint with the motes turning

in a slanted beam—O sing
the slow schoolboy's daydream
counting them in.

A Photograph of Fade Street, Dublin, 1878

The exposure, half a minute? Enough for light's breath
to cloud the glass with this narrow
Georgian canyon: dark fanlights

above dark doors, sash windows raised
while the far end assumes its name, greys
to a smoky membrane.

Steady as a gramophone needle behind his tripod,
the afternoon swirling about him,
time's pupil concentrates on

the cogs and gears. Three girls perched on a kerb
will be restless smears; two boys
sitting on a doorstep may take

if they keep staring, contracted in the same hard gaze
as their grown ups', two men in bowlers,
huddled on the next step.

Opposite, nearer, the pair of women who stand
talking with a third (held sharp
in her street-level window)

sway themselves into ghosts with a pale-faced lad
flickering from a doorway.
Others, too fast, walk

through the boxed walls, empty themselves up steps,
withdraw—an old man tapping the pane
gone, a cat in the railings—

children who whirr, sparrow across the street—

Warmer

*'We have learned nothing
in twelve thousand years.'*
— Picasso

Let us pray to
the first O

the first thought-
pebble's echo

opening wings
in the dark walls,

to Lascaux's mouldy
torch-lit halls,

the slendered, rippling
Falling Cow

(falling, flying—
who's to know?)

her hind legs coiled
her tiny head's

pincer-horns
as fine as braid,

line of her elegant
humped shoulder

traceable spine
of the herd: older,

warmer, warmer . . .
all we may get:

clouded mirrors
tower of our breath.

Plain Song

An uncalled-for
refrain—
curtain-call—

the tall
windowpanes
swish rain.

False Memory

It flashes back like an outtake: my nine-year-old flight
down a lengthening dim corridor,
those quiet words spoken by the doctor

snapping at my feet: 'I can circumcise you now, if you like.'
A joke, a grown-up bite
that stuck in my throat. Days later they put me under

and I woke to find my little man wearing a white
turban. But my mother,
what did she think of the doctor who played with fear?

'You're dreaming ... not on your life.... what do you take me for?'
But there is that soured daylight—
Stephen's Green, his surgery on the first floor.

My mother is out of the frame, but the young doctor
(pale and bearded, remember?)
sits there, feigning surprise, still holding his knife.

Naylor's Cove

One night you stumbled down to the cold shingle
to scream *fuck death* at the sea
(derelict concrete changing rooms gaping behind you)
as if this could abort the journey.

Months later, across the water, in the blank
aftermath, while she took a nap,
you watched grey squirrels skitter up and down
the skinny overgrown pines.

This is to nothing, to no one, an ocean, a merman
thrashing its tail—a boy
who would now be almost thirteen. Atomised eyes
level and look straight through

your own, unfocusing, till you know nothing but the air
that stares you so thoroughly out.

Skull

We stole it for a day, to photograph—
the dead tree, the shingled beach—

as if it needed a back-story,
was failing to speak.

Bicycle Seat
Bull's Head
Bull-Leap
—*Picasso, 1942*

Here's an answer—
slim-skulled, playful, austere,

clear as the nose—
to a problem no one posed:

how to release the bull
from the bicycle

so handlebar horns offer
a leap, charged with laughter.

Portraits of a Grouse-Beater, 1975

Your line advances over the Colonel's moor,
to scare up a fluster of wings (*go Back! go Back!*)
and wave them towards the expensive tweed, the dogs.

∼

Lunch with other beaters: sandwiches, beer.
Reaching for a can of Tennants, see your hand
close over the girl on the can, *Heather*, in pink.

∼

But you came to find the hard-paying, hard-hatted work.
A roustabout on the rigs. A roust-a-what?
Something to do with chains that can rip an arm off.

∼

In the cockpit of the jeep with the Yorkshire ex-Angel.
His grown-up tash and sideburns. He flips his lighter
and a sleepy moth goes up, then down in flames.

∼

Barely aware of the signals you send out.
The Glasgow bootboy (tidy and short, tats
on his Popeye forearms) refuses to meet your eyes.

∼

Laughing, he 'accidentally' spills his whiskey
on your grimy jeans. So, laughing, you pour yours
into his lap, his knife-creased Oxford Bags.

∼

Your poems and drawings: doodles in the margins
of doodles, a diary of loose ends. The marginal god
of fools, drunks and dossers watches over you.

∼

He is up before you can blink, head-butting, thrashing,
screams, as they drag him off and hold him back,
he'll take you on bare-handed: '. . . you can have the axe!'

∼

A cooling hearth. Glasgow has gone to bed,
and the others, except for Yorkshire who quietly begins
to try to explain exactly how worthless you are.

∼

You keep schtum. What is he trying to push you towards?
Self-knowledge? Suicide? You can always use
more of the first, travelling far too light.

∼

So dreamy you never figured to sign on
in Edinburgh—have somewhere to bring a girl,
breathe on a bedsit pane, patch out the world.

∼

Found in the heather: the bleached skull of a mouse,
a brown-red feather, a dirty tuft of wool—
sewn to your army jacket like a badge.

Found Landscape
i.m. Desmond Stephenson

A late work, one of his last.
Oil on board: evening, low
slate clouds, moss-dark mountains,
one of them sporting a deft flick

of mercury light—a road.
It was taken down, put aside
when we found strange stars, holes
freckling a corner of sky—

lost in storage. Crossing those
mountains, years later, I looked
and looked again: a pale lane
scudded off downhill, rose

and narrowed—a broken stroke
of painterliness. We parked
where he might have set up,
his loaded brush—Payne's Grey?

Raw Sienna?—the road now
magnified, cratered with rain-filled
potholes, flash of his glasses,
restored light in his eyes.

At the Butcher's in Colmenar

A framed, blown-up photograph hangs on the wall:
the t-shirted butcher's son and his wife, on their honeymoon
in Manhattan, the towers in the background, the date:
September 10, 2001.

Behind the counter, a steel door opens: a glimpse
of pale waxy carcasses, smell so thick I could colour it
black-red: the colour of history. Outside, I breathe
warm streets, damp from a recent shower.

An old man swings past on crutches. What do I know
about history? Dawdling under a nearby orange tree—
its perfect glimmering system—I think
of reaching to pluck one.

ANDALUCÍA, 2004

At Sea
i.m. Neil O'Brien

His stated wish—to be scattered at
the Forty Foot—was carried out

with difficulty. This wasn't a day
suitably in mourning, empty.

The weather was fine, the place rife
with splashes, laughter—life

(the kind of day Neil might have sprung
into the *great sweet*, like Mulligan).

On the road above, some of us gathered
to murmur a few words,

while I kept my eyes on that rowboat
ferrying his urn to a remote

and suitable distance. I looked for
the unlidded cloud (ash poured

like water) but could make out only
something they let fall, gently

as a lifebelt.

Section
for Sam and Simon

On the other side
of the raised, blanket divide

surgeon and interns delved
into the earthworks. You held

something of ourselves together,
rocked by rough weather.

Luck was too small a word
when they found a knot in his cord,

cut and hoisted him—blood
and blue thunder, a storm-cloud

blazoning our eyes—high
in his first sky.

The Older Standing Army

Decamped some time ago, rank upon rank,
to the rooftops.

Here they lift pint pots
of evening and morning sun, and perhaps one

in ten brandishes a plant, an antique aerial or
is garlanded with a nest.

Most of them are not
speaking now, pillars of a too high, too clear

society of coos and caws, star-hammered doors,
bluegreys or anaemic

no less exhausted air.
Nevertheless, they are still organs of the snug,

coughing, whiskey-lit, smoke-signalled city, its fug
louring in low clouds.

Who else to uphold
all those burnt columns of births and deaths, the gold

worked into the old lining, the grimecoat?

One of the Houses James Joyce Lived In, Once

James Joyce ivy
on James Joyce plaque,
James Joyce pebbles
on James Joyce dash,
James Joyce knocker
on James Joyce door,
James Joyce dust
on James Joyce floor,
James Joyce windows
with James Joyce glass
waiting for James Joyce
clouds to pass.

Ghost Story

'Listen hard enough and you wake the dead.'

On an Empty Can
Rolling in the Night
a Week After Your Death
i.m. Anthony Glavin

Something scratches and scrapes
a hole in my dreamscape,

like one of your once-in-a-black-moon
distress calls to summon

a human voice. What wakes me now
is a mouthful of wind, a hollow

with nothing to tell, old friend,
unless your ghost can bend

its will, rewire the silence,
kick some kind of sense

(hard love that had no use
for the easeful half-truths)

into a can's life-in-death rattle
that cannot, should not, be still.

The Chaos Ripple

Forget the butterfly, it's a mooncold moth—
tatterdemalion wings unsettling the soft

night air—trying to bump through our windowpane
to catch, incandesce in the light of reason.

The Doctor
for Donal Costigan

Angled a penlight into the young man's eye.
Nothing. Persistent pain
can mean anything. Works in the merchant navy.
Syphilis might explain . . .

Cloud-break: sun flamed the window
and every surface—the stubbly face, the iris—
to pick out the needletip glow
that, drawn, became a split

hair of metal, a star excavated by a star.

Eclipse

A weather-darkened ball of granite, wide
as a hooped embrace, broken off
some ivied pillar. Some passers by had seen it—
drunks most likely—rolled it till the novelty
wore off. Outside our gates,

abandoned or delivered, it carried a world
of purpose. So I rolled it
over our gravel drive, around the house,
onto the patio in the back garden
where it rested, below the rockery—

something else entirely, more and more
familiarly strange. Its mottled greyness gave
a blurred corona, burning out the lawn
and garden wall, gathering waves of silence—
a moon, a fallen moon

making space in a back garden.

Night, Wind, Dead Leaves

rattle and hiss, the sound so high
it is almost a whistle,

their bodying sigh
the air of something more palpable

than passing by.

Wake

Downstairs, in our made-over sitting room,
grandmother tinkled her little brass bell at all hours.
We hired a nurse and slept through. It became normal.
That night grandmother called

my name (the nurse told me afterwards), till she settled
into her deathbed, the one we waked her in—
a rearranged bouquet tucked into crisp-shadowed folds.
For two nights, we slept with the dead.

On the second, something woke me—a dream bell?
descended a dream, to her door.
Held there, almost unable to turn the handle,
I opened it enough to be startled

by our cat curled in its chair,
dead-still, but for its wide-awake, breathing stare.

A Chest of Drawers

The bedsit you *didn't* rent in a net-curtained suburb,
landlady below, basin lording over the bed.

The vigil: at your aunt's full-roomed Victorian mirror
waiting for your stoned reflection to move a hair.

Those tea-chests lined with foil: aromatic emptiness
a larynx for what got left, its unsettled hiss.

The *Friendly* or *Safety* that could Swiss-Army-knife into anything:
hash-pipe, doll's drawer, pocket version of the I Ching . . .

The walnut writing desk with the false drawer
and a puffed-up Rorschach face in the smoky veneer.

Your job in a nursing home, sweeping each spotless room.
The stiff laid out in his suit. Your 'excuse me' to no one.

Doors of the piss-smelling lift sliding shut before
you discovered dark was in order.

Outside, In
for G.W.

Across the road, tall chestnuts framed
a taller building (white-barred windows)—

a wing of Saint John of God's: nervous
breakdowns, schizophrenics, depressives—

the man I watched, from our front door,
slowly climb through two bent bars

in one of the lower windows, to stand
in his rumpled suit on an outhouse roof.

An interval, some breath to draw
on his makeshift patio, before

two bare-armed men in tunics made
the same entrance and carefully,

very carefully, persuaded him
to climb back in.
                    Decades later,

a gentle, candid friend (who had done
time there more than once) told me

how it feels to discover your door
lacks a handle.

Crest

On a drystone wall a stoat
stops, as if taking

its own pulse: rampant
heraldic stand-in for

the whole family—stone,
earth, water, fire . . .

fluidly gone,
          so
sky readjusts to sky,

grass to grass,
drystone to dry stone.

Pocket Venus

Unearthed: a bulbous root—
staring belly, tiny arms draped like a stole
above heavyweight breasts, bowed head
cauled in the crocheted cap of her hair—she floats

ice ages, huddled nights
on the banks of the Danube twenty-five millennia ago.
The earth hath bubbles, as the water has . . .

that break in a smile, in this
blown-up doll? quivering prayer?
                                    Summer,
she'll turn up, bright as a tulip—
that girl rounding the corner
of Mountjoy Square—

gravity's joy in the bounce of her breast, the worldwide
sway of her hip.

There's Probably No God. Now Stop Worrying and Enjoy Your Life
—*Ad by The Atheist Bus Campaign*

Not only
is there
probably
no god,
but this is
probably
not your bus.

Breasts

Something of him never did the hard paths,
the choppy waves, the maths.

Instead, he aspired to those
territories of softness—

O and O—as if this
is where every good swooner goes.

Fruit Bats in Sydney
for Delia and Richard

1. Evening, Port Elizabeth

Four stories up, at the appointed hour,
we watched it begin: a scatter of sooty flakes

rose from the softlit city (an upside down chandelier)
outriders' pterodactyl wings

smuttering, near.

2. Afternoon, Botanic Park

On the barer branches clumps
of burn-coloured fruit unhooked to hang-glide

blue gaps. Their shit anointed the paths, a loamy
counterpoint to the bustle and bloom,

invisible caves to step through.

On the Sky Road to Malaga

We pulled in when we saw that leaning house
in a layby on a high bend. The peaked roof sat
soberly on two walls canted sideways.

Too recent to be called a ruin: a half-squashed,
bungalow-shaped tunnel (maybe the earth
slid or some trucker fell asleep for good).

House hinged on its own buckled moment.
House looking away from the sea's whitegold pane.
House holding the off-kilter ghost of itself.

We circled with cameras, tried to unlock some new
angle: a white-robed mountain and the moon
cosily at home, a roof over their heads.

Nothing we sighted through that crooked frame
fitted better than what it was furnished with:
baked earth, scrubby weeds, yellowing newspapers.

House shuttered and haunted by fresh air.
House that says No, go now, gun the motor.
House around the corner from Malaga.

New Year's

I ram bottles into the bank,
listening for the weak *tink!*
or the solid, gratifying smash
of a breakthrough, a full-blown wish.

Critic

I should have forgotten that pet shop
off some back street, somewhere on the north side.
Dim, nicotine light, salty-sweet smells
of dogbiscuit, straw, big sacks of grain and seed.

What am I doing there, lost in the usual?
Startled out of it by a hoarse, old-woman voice
shouting—*Gedoffdatchair!*
I spin round. Nobody there

but the shopkeeper, his mustached smile.
—*Gedoffdatchair!* Now I see it
in a cage hanging from the ceiling: a restless crow.
No, 'a mynah.' Imagine bringing home that

cracked voice for a pet. Where would it go?
Here, here in my ear—Get off that chair.

Stopwatch

Over fifty now, one of those joggers who pass,
heads down—hard shins and soft knees—eyes on the grass,

I crank myself into old age, hold to the thin
muddied track made by runners, that keeps grass down.

Here I come, round and around—the tip of a second hand
on a blank green clock, marking what will unwind

lap by lap, the lagging flesh on its beat
from what will escape it—spirited, hard-soled, fleet.

Later Days
after Philip Larkin

Having followed them to the foothills
of heart attack and cancer country where
the ground lurches, see-saws

I'm surprised to discover (squinting
through all those splashes of fear)
the relief of another one over

and done—brief open/shut book—
the plunge towards extinction (still
too terrifying to be real)

more and more natural: glints
of foam, mica flecks, filaments
from the gorgeous roar

of light's birthday party
where sea was land, land sea.

Three Riddles and a Limerick*

Sometimes I'm a knife,
sometimes a feather,
sometimes a bulldozer.
Before I came along
trees couldn't find their tongues.
Now the forests are full of whispers.

～

You might be pleased to see me
or find me too honest for words.
But come close, breathe on me
and I'll vanish obediently.

～

It is we who have to bear the weight
of every creature walking the earth.
We are glad only one of these
sees fit to imprison us
in soft coffins,
keeping us in the dark.

～

There once was a boy called Robartes
whose doctor insisted 'No Smarties!
or you'll grow up to perne
in a gyre with Aherne
and the rest of those high-talking hearties.'

* Answers to riddles can be found in *Notes*

After Li Po

Time now. Two drunks veer
to the end of the old pier,
piss, then disappear.

The Far Side
for Ronan and Raif

Having dandered along the train-tracks
this far, we pushed ahead
into that blacker, narrower
tunnel the day could not thread.

Maybe two hundred yards,
till our half-sleeping resistance
about-turned, repointed us backwards
with nothing to pocket but this:

daylight shrunk to a half moon,
an evening star—poking the lair
of something whose oily skin
we had begun to wear.

Dark Mutter

Every thing tends
to its own ends.

Dream

With Seamus Heaney, in a deserted sitting room
off a busy university-corridor. We settle on
an old sofa. He takes a cushion, places it
on my lap, plumps it, nestles
his white-crowned head
and is asleep.

Lookout

The lowest branch a bar to help you climb
into the V, then heave through the square hole
in the floor: a nest of plywood, forgotten doors
my cousin banged together one day, for years
cradled in our tallest apple tree. That's me

on the roof's warped sheet of corrugated iron,
standing under the sun, staring away
over neighboring trees, roofs, fields, to make out
Howth Head's cagy embrace, and just below it,
a stubborn flake of ultramarine. I grip

bendy branches: knuckly, sap-green cookers
(too bitter to sink your teeth in, too many to harvest)
and throw my weight from one foot to the other
till the whole shapeless vessel creaks and sways.

The Last Wolf in Ireland

*Pray you, no more of this; 'tis like the howling
of Irish wolves against the moon.*
                              — As You Like It

The last wolf in Ireland

Was hunted down, caught and skinned like the others.
Was neither seen nor heard.
Was heard howl one last time, at a slip of a moon
blacked out in cloud.
Was never even rumoured as it skirted the nets
of history and symbol.

Was glimpsed once, fifty years after
all wolves were declared gone—
a creak in the evening, the lean mask's
paler stillness, between what was left of the oaks—
by a horseman who crossed himself
in fear or reverence or both
and spoke of it to no one.

Was anywhere, nowhere, a face in a folded pack,
a title searching for a poem
facing extinction.

'Don't End with History or the Sea'

a poet warns us, or you'll make each thing
'sound like everything else.'

Here, above Blackrock, everything slopes
to that great, warped lens.
Buildings stand in the way, borrow the light.

Stars, of course, and mountains, heavens and hells
can rattle like anything else.

Days, nights, when there is nowhere better to look,
I sometimes drive there, park at a low wall
in Sandycove or Seapoint,

to write or just sit, long enough to take home
equilibrium, one little bucket of history
slopping gently on whatever scales

register these things.

Handholds

1.

Spiral. We set it down where we can, a ripple
on tombs, brooches, stones, the pattern of holes
in a soup-strainer. Sacred and inscrutable, the line
has got under our skin. The scrolled-up symbol, awake,
begins to uncoil.

∼

Though we've housed them soundly, the dead,
their voices reach us, restlessness
of wind grass tree cloud—words
on the tips of their tongues.

∼

Safe in the firelit night.
Safe in the sunlit wood.
Safe as a well-fenced field.
Safe as our guarded cattle.
Safe as a crannog, a ring-fort.

Still, sometimes we tremble
like a wind-blown nest in the bramble.

2.

New geometry everywhere now.
The worldly raindrop, cloud-cliffs,
night and day are designed
by a different architect.
The chorus of old names has sunk
to the dark at the heart of a daisy,
or they loiter by the old wells, stand
like shadows behind each grassblade.

They have only stepped back a little,
out of the sphere of this bright new
magic with its hard-edged symbols,
the sun + moon spiked by a cross.
Silent men sit in the woods,
not working but busy, their quill-tips
blackened with holly-juice, beetling

as if the sweet breeze from a blackbird
should fit into laddery lines,
as if you could thread the wind,
as if this god could be tugged out
with a jewelled chain of capital letters . . .

∼

See, in the valleys at dusk,
pockets of glimmers, licks
of candle-light at a window.
Dreamy as the drift of sparks
that catches, for a few seconds,
in the throat of a chimney.

∼

Now we hear it, the voice of money
making its own rosary,
fish-eyed, splash-headed kings,
dud bells, a trickle of clinks,
metal talking to metal.

3.

Boats broaden, sewers
add their tongues
to the black pool,
reflections climb into glass

∼

Then, they are moving the furniture
again, rifling under

the road's carpet: not there.
area railings, fanlights, the blotched greys
in the old photographs —

a whinny, a cough, silence that gently flicked
its carthorse ears into the 1960s

and on: dandelioned yards dragged out
like untidy drawers, ransacked —

flameshadowed brick, a child rolling a tyre
as big as herself to the bonfire —

wallpapered gaps, a fireplace, a shirt on a chair —

a city half-dressed in a rush
patting its disappeared pockets.

∼

Hill Street: below the church tower
the graveyard now a playground squeals
and shrieks. The steel tube slide

flashes a welt of sun.
Disciplined, displaced stones
line the walls. There is nowhere
left to lean.

~

There: the voices thrown
from Thingmote's mound

Here: moved earth, the grind
of gears on Nassau Street

There: what netted the names
in the map's blood vessels

Here: names to be given:
Skateboard Alley, Fr. Noise Quay,
Out Of Our Heads Walk

There: footholds, the splash of feet
on the hurdle ford

Here: old ladders in a skip,
new holds, rungs in the air

There: Pale walls, the beerbarrel
clatter of weaponry

Here: a soiled pink blanket
in a doorway, a nation at the gates,
real estate

4.

River your fine silts
alluvial alphabets known
to brewers, gulls, mullet
river splitting the grey
ice age, its flashy
bracelets of traffic,
river strung with bridges,
intravenous river gone
under the skin with rain's
needling voices, river now
as then, speaking the glacial
unfinished sentence

∼

flutter of war plague fire
where fingers of forest
oak groves, bare-headed hills
in the before-dawn blue—
a shudder of wind in the leaves
maps breathing and rustling
whitefire gulls in the squares
tongues in the old bells bonging
smell of piss in an alley
cranes turning like weathercocks
turfsmoke blown across
bricky and glassy centuries
corners gateways laneways
backstreets of the sea

Departures
Long after the Irish (A.D. 600–1200)

COLUM CILLE'S DERRY

Beyond doubt, I love Derry,
so calm, bright and airy—

on each hill, every street,
angels adjusting the light.

THE BELL

Melodious bell-notes roll
onto the windy night,

to comfort and console
more than women might.

OISÍN REMEMBERS

Those days, my hair was gold—
a torc, a sunstruck wave.
Crowned with frost now, I'm cold,
nothing for wind to love.

Better to have hair smoked
a raven's uncouth colour
than these stiffened, clipped
wings of winter.

Days when I'd dazzle a girl
then pick her up like a feather
are daydreams, fairydust hurled
over dark water.

THE HOSTING

It is a king's work, this hosting
of all of Adam's seed,
and yet is it no work, nothing
at all, and it proceeds.

No sooner do we know
than we study to forget
where the hosting goes—
no one is ready yet.

When you are called forth,
if you refuse to leave,
in whose house, whose fort
will you stand siege?

PAYMENT IN KIND

He'll never trade you a horse
for a beautiful, thoroughbred verse.

He will offer you something hollow
as his heart: an old cow.

Among Trees

As I bend to my book,
a blackbird opens its beak—

his yellow note runs through the shade:
something else to praise.

And now the cuckoo, clear
and deep, utters his prayer.

I am happy here. Go easy,
Lord, on my Judgement Day.

The Yes Man

When I nod among my seniors
they are glad to see I am serious.

When I am with the young
I'm their wildest song.

The Terror

Tonight, the wind is the terror:
it claws at the waves' white hair.

No fear of iron-headed icemen steadily
slicing the Irish Sea.

Memo

Remember the hour
when a real foot stands on real earth—it leaves the print
of a centaur,
a whiff of horse-sweat and wild mint.

You might start there.

Notes

WARMER
Special thanks to Ian Duhig, who reminded me of Picasso's response to the cave art in Lascaux.

A CHEST OF DRAWERS
Friendly and *Safety* were the two most popular types of matchbox available in Ireland.

OUTSIDE, IN
The old St. John of God's, Stillorgan, Co. Dublin.

POCKET VENUS
The so-called 'Venus of Willendorf.' Italicised line is from Macbeth: Banquo, on seeing The Three Weird Sisters vanish.

THREE RIDDLES AND A LIMERICK
The first two lines of the Limerick were supplied by Séan Lysaght, during a discussion about Yeats's collection 'Robartes And The Dancer'. I have been reliably informed that Yeats (on a BBC recording) pronounced 'Robartes' to rhyme with 'hearts'.

The answers to the three riddles: the wind, your reflection in a mirror, feet.

'DON'T END WITH HISTORY OR THE SEA'
Kenneth Koch.

DEPARTURES
From cribs and translations of the old Irish (A.D. 600 to 1200) by Kuno Meyer, Gerard Murphy, David Greene and Frank O'Connor. The originals are all by Anon, with the possible exception of 'The Yes Man' (titled 'All Things To All Men' by Murphy), which has been ascribed to Mo Ling.